iMath
Readers

Winning the Game:
Putting Miles in Their Place

by Renata Brunner-Jass

Content Consultant
David T. Hughes
Mathematics Curriculum Specialist

NORWOODHOUSE PRESS
Chicago, IL

Norwood House Press
PO Box 316598
Chicago, IL 60631

For information regarding Norwood House Press, please visit our website at
www.norwoodhousepress.com or call 866-565-2900.

Special thanks to: Heidi Doyle
Production Management: Six Red Marbles
Editors: Linda Bullock and Kendra Muntz
Printed in Heshan City, Guangdong, China. 208N—012013

Library of Congress Cataloging–in-Publication Data

Brunner-Jass, Renata.

  Winning the game: putting miles in their place/by Renata Brunner-Jass ;
  content consultant David Hughes, mathematics curriculum specialist.
  pages cm.—(iMath)

  Audience: 10–12
  Audience: Grade 4 to 6

  Summary: "The mathematical concepts of place value and integers are
  introduced as students design a board game in which they must keep
  track of distance with addition and multiplication. Readers learn about
  expanded notation and place value charts. Includes a discover activity,
  history connection, and mathematical vocabulary introduction"—Provided
  by publisher.

Includes bibliographical references and index.

ISBN 978-1-59953-567-8 (library edition : alk. paper)
ISBN 978-1-60357-536-2 (ebook)

1. Place value (Mathematics)—Juvenile literature. 2. Numeration—Juvenile literature. I. Title.

QA141.3.B78 2013
513.5—dc23
2012023952

CONTENTS

Note to Caregivers:

Throughout this book, many questions are posed to the reader. Some are open-ended and ask what the reader thinks. Discuss these questions with your child and guide him or her in thinking through the possible answers and outcomes. There are also questions posed which have a specific answer. Encourage your child to read through the text to determine the correct answer. Most importantly, encourage answers grounded in reality while also allowing imaginations to soar. Information to help support you as you share the book with your child is provided in the back in the **Additional Notes** section.

Bold words are defined in the glossary in the back of the book.

4

Go the Extra Mile

Each year, Mr. Rivera, our teacher, asks his students to create a special geography project. This year, Deon, Ramona, and I worked together to make ours. It's a board game. We call it *Go the Extra Mile*.

We glued a map of North America to a piece of cardboard. This is our game board. Then, we made 150 travel cards. Each travel card describes a travel adventure. Players earn or lose miles, depending on their adventures.

The winner is the first person to reach 5,000 miles. There's one more rule, too. Every card has a geography question. Players who answer a geography question correctly earn 100 free miles. If they answer incorrectly, they lose 100 miles.

The day our project was due, Mr. Rivera asked us to play our game for the class. He joined us. Who traveled 5,000 miles before anyone else? The answer is in the cards.

Choose the method you like best for keeping score. Then, follow along as we see the winner and losers of the first official game of *Go the Extra Mile*.

Who Will Win?

We talked about the different ways we could keep score as we played. That is the only way to know who wins. We thought any one of these four ways might work well.

Idea 1: Each player could draw a **tally chart** like the one below. With each round, the player could add or subtract tally marks to show the new score.

What is this player's score so far?

Miles	Tenths of a Mile
卌 卌	ⅠⅠⅠⅠ

Do you think keeping tally charts will be a good way to keep score? Why or why not?

Idea 2: Each player could use **blocks** or other objects to represent different values. Players could use decimal blocks to show tenths. Then, players could add and subtract blocks at the end of each round, **regrouping** when necessary. Regrouping is using place value to think of a number in a different way. For example, 12 ones can be regrouped as 1 ten and 2 ones.

What is this player's score so far?

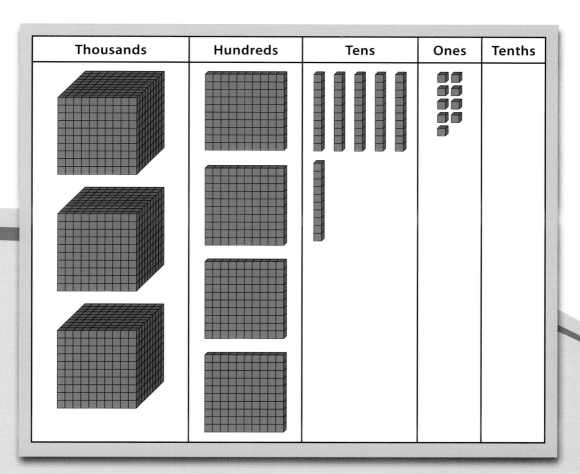

Thousands	Hundreds	Tens	Ones	Tenths

Do you think using blocks to represent numbers would be a good way to keep score? Why or why not?

Idea 3: Players could write each whole number in **expanded notation.** Then, they could add or subtract. For example, if a player traveled 1,123.5 miles in one trip and 834.5 miles in a second trip, the player could write:

$$
\begin{array}{r}
(1 \times 1,000) + (1 \times 100) + (2 \times 10) + (3 \times 1) \\
+ \qquad\qquad\qquad (8 \times 100) + (3 \times 10) + (4 \times 1) \\
\hline
1,000 + (9 \times 100) + (5 \times 10) + (7 \times 1)
\end{array}
$$

Then, the player could add the tenths and regroup if necessary.

$$
\begin{array}{r}
0.5 \text{ mile from the first trip} \\
+ \; 0.5 \text{ mile from the second trip} \\
\hline
1 \text{ mile in all}
\end{array}
$$

What is this player's score so far?

Do you think using expanded notation would be a good way to keep score? Why or why not?

Idea 4: We came up with a fourth idea. Players could draw **place-value charts** like these.

This player started with 722.8 miles. Then, he traveled 314.5 more miles. Did the player add correctly?

+/−	Thousands	Hundreds	Tens	Ones	.	Tenths
	1			1		
	7	2	2	.		8
+		3	1	4	.	5
	1	0	3	7	.	3

The same player lost 100 miles when he couldn't answer the question on his card. What is the player's score now?

+/−	Thousands	Hundreds	Tens	Ones	.	Tenths
	0	10				
	1	0	3	7	.	3
−		1	0	0	.	0

Do you think using place-value charts would be a good way to keep score? Why or why not?

Materials
- 6 blank cubes or 6 number cubes
- masking tape
- marker
- paper and pencil

Rolling Operations

Let's say that you're getting ready to play our geography game. But first you want to practice your **operation** skills, such as addition and subtraction. There are many ways you can add and subtract.

Gather a set of six plain blocks or six number cubes. Cover each side of the blocks with masking tape. Write one-digit numbers on each side of five cubes. Draw a period on each side of the last cube to represent a decimal point.

Roll the cubes. You can roll them all at once. Or, you can roll them one at a time.

When the cubes come to rest, put them side by side to create a number with one decimal place.

Then, roll the cubes again to create a second number.

What do you notice about the numbers you roll? How will you decide which number is larger?

Use the numbers you roll to practice two operations, addition and subtraction.

Start with addition. Decide which method you will use to find the sum of the miles.

- a tally chart
- base-ten blocks and decimal blocks
- expanded form, or notation
- a place-value chart

How many miles did you travel in all?

If you used a place-value chart, challenge yourself to check your work by using the opposite operation. Subtract the lesser **addend**, or number being added, from the **sum**, or total. If your answer matches the greater addend, your answer is correct.

Now, use the numbers you rolled to practice subtraction. If you decide to use a place-value chart, remember to put the larger value on top of the lesser value. Also remember that you may need to regroup.

If you use a place-value chart, challenge yourself to check your work by using the opposite operation. Add the **difference**, or answer to the subtraction problem, to the **subtrahend**. The subtrahend is the number you subtract. If your answer matches the **minuend**, or the number you subtracted from, your answer is correct.

Each of us agrees to help each other keep score. We decide to use place-value charts. Which method will you use to check our scorekeeping? Get your paper and pencil out now. The game is about to begin!

Mr. Rivera starts the first round. Mr. Rivera selected this travel card:

> You are a huge rodeo fan. So, you drive 199.8 miles from Kalispell, Montana, to the Calgary Stampede in Alberta. What country are you in?

"Canada," says Mr. Rivera, adding his miles. "And I do like rodeos," he adds. What is his score?

Next, Ramona takes a card. It says:

> You travel 188.2 miles northwest from Albuquerque, New Mexico, to Four Corners. Which four states meet at Four Corners?

Ramona pipes up, "Arizona, New Mexico, Utah, and Colorado." That's correct. So, she earns 100 bonus miles, too. How many miles does she have in all?

This is the current marker at the exact Four Corners meeting point.

Deon is a geography genius. I think his parents replaced baby books with a world atlas. Otherwise, how could he know so much?

Deon's card says:

> You fly 1,373.7 miles from Los Angeles to Houston. Then, you wait to board another plane to travel 1,276.4 more miles to Jackson Hole, Wyoming. Jackson Hole is at the base of what mountain range?

"The Cascades," Deon says. Mr. Rivera shakes his head. "No, it's the Tetons."

"Of course!" Deon says. "What was I thinking?"

These mountains are part of the Teton Range.

Deon loses 100 miles. But he still has a huge score!

How many miles does Deon have before he subtracts 100 miles?

What is Deon's total after he subtracts 100 miles?

It is my turn next. All I can think about is Deon's score. I really want a card like his, but I get this one.

> The Iditarod Great Sled Race is 975 miles long. You and your dogs have 325.5 more miles to go before you reach the end of the trail.

My miles don't come close to Deon's. In fact, I'm only about $\frac{2}{3}$ of the way along the trail. I'm going to have to subtract to find my total. And that's going to require some regrouping. How many miles have I traveled so far?

I finish reading the card, hoping I can earn the bonus miles.

In 1925, a disease called diphtheria struck Nome. Airplanes couldn't fly through a blizzard to deliver medicine. So, mushers organized a relay of dog-sled teams to reach the sick. The Iditarod Great Sled Race marks this historic event each year. In what state is the race held?

"Alaska!" I call out.

"You're right, B.J.," Mr. Rivera says to me with a big smile. "That gives you 100 bonus miles."

What's my score now?

Did You Know?

Dog-sled racers are called mushers. The word may have come from early French explorers, who used the word *marcher* to mean "to go," and the word *marchent* to mean "let's walk." English settlers probably picked up the words and changed them to make them easier to say.

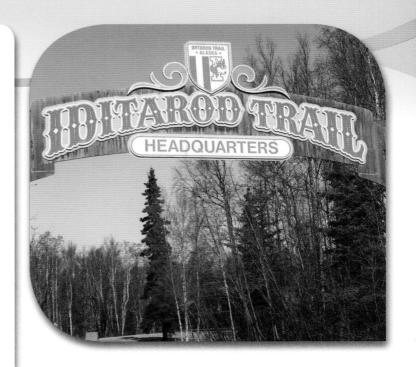

Looking Back

Before we start the next round, we put our scores in a bar graph to make them easy to compare.

Mr. Rivera	299.8 miles
Ramona	288.2 miles
Deon	2,550.1 miles
B.J.	749.5 miles

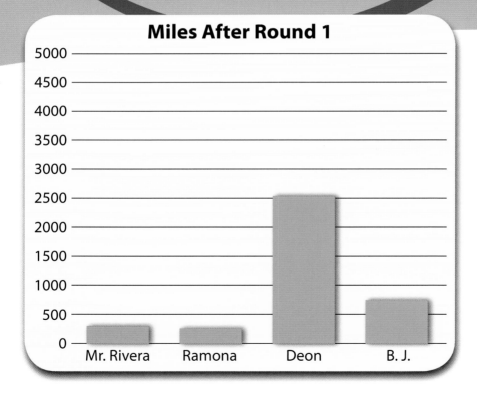

Miles After Round 1

How many more miles does Deon need to win the game?

Round 2

Round 2 begins. Mr. Rivera takes a card. He smiles widely. "Another international adventure," he says.

> You travel 67.2 miles on a bus from Mexico City to Piedra Herrada, where you enter a sanctuary for millions of butterflies that migrate from Canada to Central Mexico. What butterfly have you come to see?

Mr. Rivera smiles. "It's the Monarch butterfly, or mariposa monarca," he says.

What is Mr. Rivera's score now, including his bonus miles?

What's the Word?

Imagine millions of butterflies spending the winter together in warmer climates. Learn more about the biology of these insects and see amazing photographs in Kathryn Lasky's book called *Monarchs*.

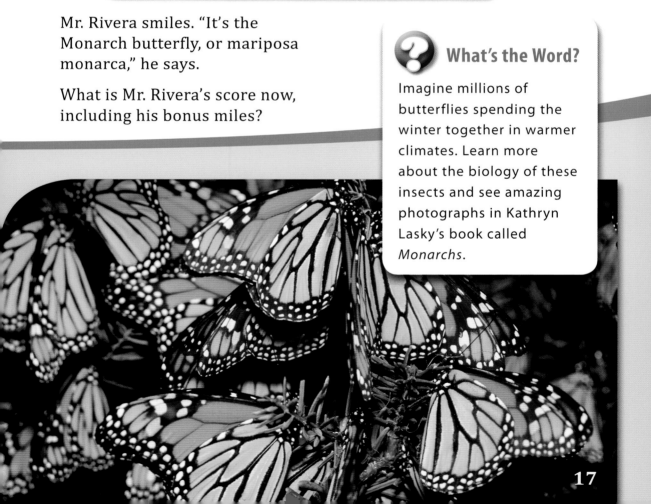

Ramona goes next. She needs a long trip to catch up with Deon. In fact, we all need a long trip if we are going to catch up to Deon.

We listen as Ramona reads her card.

> You grab your snowboard, a stiff brush, and extra sunscreen. You travel 1,516.7 miles to a park in Oregon. This park is the first of its kind in the world. Don't expect snow. What will you be sliding down in the park?

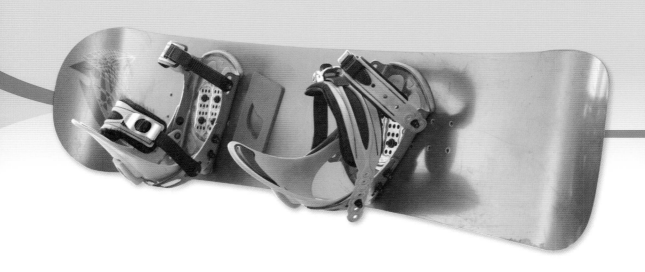

Suddenly, I am confused. But Ramona grins. "Sand dunes," she says.

"If you're riding sand," I ask, "why do you use a snowboard?"

"Well, a snowboard can do the same job. But people use special sandboards, too. Sandboards are harder and slide more easily."

She plays several sports and knows about a lot of other sports, too.

What is Ramona's total now?

Now it's Deon's turn again. He reads his card aloud.

> You fly 171.9 miles from Las Vegas, Nevada, to a horse ranch near the Grand Canyon. While you're there, you take a helicopter ride down into the canyon and put a raft in the river. What river flows through the canyon?

"The Colorado River," he says, adding 100 bonus miles to his sum. What's Deon's score now?

"Did you know," I say, "that rivers are rated from 1 to 6? A Grade 1 river has a few rough parts and is good for beginning rafters. But Grade 6 rivers can be deadly."

"That's cool," Ramona says. "I want to go rafting one day." Deon and Mr. Rivera agree.

The Colorado River flows through the Grand Canyon.

I can hardly wait to go again.

> Your team of geographers follows the Lewis and Clark trail. You travel 3,700 miles from St. Charles, Missouri, to the coast, where the Columbia River empties into the ocean. Which ocean is it?

"Yahoo!" I call out. "I get 3,700 miles in one play!"

Made in 2004, this U.S. postage stamp marks the bicentennial of Lewis and Clark's journey.

Unfortunately, I am so excited that I blurt out the first ocean name I think of. "The Atlantic," I call out.

Instantly, I know what I've done. I shake my head in disbelief. "It's the Pacific," I say the second time. "I know I've lost 100 miles. But that's okay. 3,700 – 100 still leaves me with 3,600 miles. I'm way ahead!"

What's my score now?

Looking Back

Before we start the next round, we update our bar graph.

Mr. Rivera	467.0 miles
Ramona	1,904.9 miles
Deon	2,822.0 miles
B.J.	4,349.5 miles

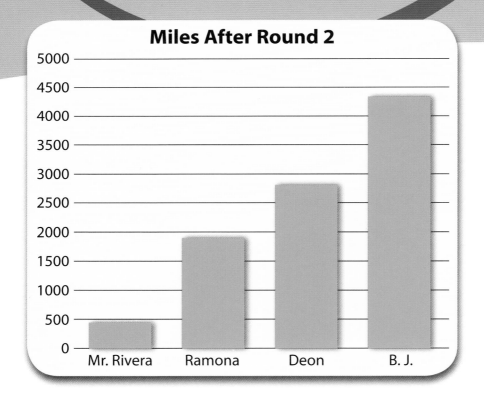

How many more miles do I need to win the game?

Mr. Rivera's next card says:

> Your hike begins at Springer Mountain, Georgia. Five months later, you reach the end of the trail at Katahdin, Maine. You have walked 2,180 miles through 14 states. What trail did you follow?

"Why, it's the Appalachian Trail, of course," Mr. Rivera says. His score soars. How many miles does he have now?

Ramona is next.

> You travel 1,565.8 miles to visit Niagara Falls. The Niagara River forms a boundary between Canada and the United States and connects two of the Great Lakes. What are the two lakes?

I have no idea. But Ramona seems to. Her lips move silently, as she puts up one finger at a time. I realize she's counting the lakes in her head. "Lake Erie and Lake Ontario," she says.

Wow! Ramona is really good at this game.

How many miles does Ramona have now?

Ramona is suddenly a lot closer to winning. I wait to hear what Deon's card says.

> You drive 89 miles from Burlington, Vermont, to Bretton Woods, New Hampshire. You purchase a ticket to ride a cog railway to the top of New England's tallest peak. What is the peak?

"Only 89 miles!" I think to myself. I'm even closer to winning! I try to hide my enthusiasm.

"Mt. Washington is the tallest peak in New England," Deon says.

Mr. Rivera says Deon is correct. I'm impressed. I had never heard of Mt. Washington before.

What is Deon's score now?

At last! It's my turn again. Will this be the winning moment? I read the card and frown.

> You walk 2.2 miles from your hotel to take a tour at 1600 Pennsylvania Avenue. What are you going to tour?

Only 2.2 miles, I think silently. Still, the question is easy. I am glad to have an extra 100 miles.

"I'm touring the White House in Washington, D.C."

What is my total score now?

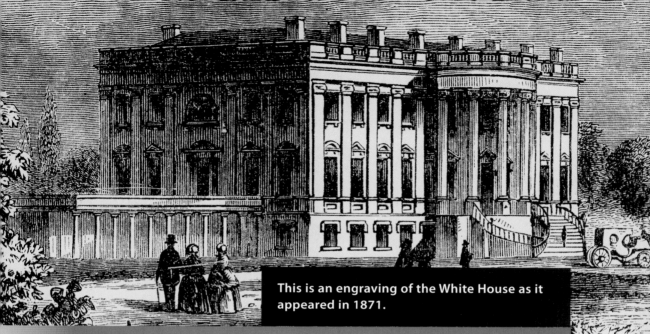

This is an engraving of the White House as it appeared in 1871.

CONNECTING TO HISTORY

The White House

President George Washington, working with city planner Pierre L'Enfant, chose 1600 Pennsylvania Avenue as the official site for the president's home. The first stone to become part of the White House was laid in 1792.

President John and Abigail Adams were the first residents. They moved into the home in 1800, before it was finished.

The current White House is not the same home that John and Abigail Adams lived in. Presidents who followed made changes to the building.

Today, the White House has 132 rooms and 35 bathrooms. All together, there are 412 doors, 147 windows, and 28 fireplaces. And so people can move up and down all six levels, there are 8 staircases and 3 elevators.

Now, I want to figure out how many more miles I need to win the game. So, this time, I use a place-value chart to subtract.

I need 548.3 miles to reach 5,000 miles. I might do that in a single round. Or, it could take a lot longer.

Looking Back

Before we start Round 4, we update our bar graph.

Mr. Rivera	2,747.0 miles
Ramona	3,570.7 miles
Deon	3,011.0 miles
B.J.	4,451.7 miles

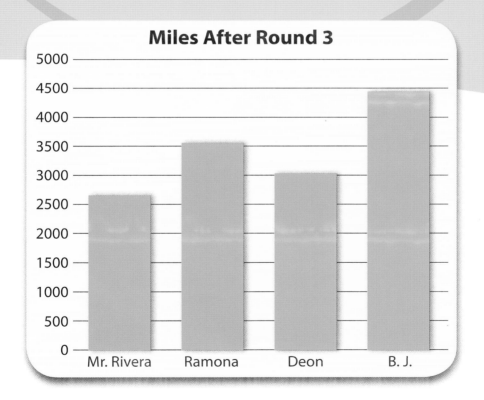

I still have a good lead. I may even win in the next round, but it's too soon to tell. One good card could send any one of us soaring past 5,000 miles.

Round 4

Mr. Rivera takes a card to begin Round 4.

> You board a train in Chicago. After traveling 480.1 miles, you get off the train in Memphis. You spend the night in the town where rock and roll was born. The next morning, you return to the train station and travel 356.8 more miles to the "Big Easy." It's the largest city in Louisiana. What city is it?

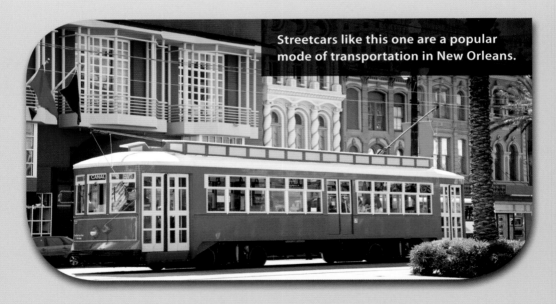

Streetcars like this one are a popular mode of transportation in New Orleans.

Mr. River smiles. "It's New Orleans," he says, earning 100 bonus miles.

How many miles does Mr. Rivera have now?

This direction sign is posted on a beach in Key West, Florida.

It is Ramona's turn next. This is what her card says.

You drive 1,087.7 miles from Newark, New Jersey, to Miami, Florida. In Miami, you are close to the overseas highway that connects to Key West, Florida. At one point, Key West is only 90 miles from a Spanish-speaking island nation. What is this nation?

Ramona answers, "Cuba," faster than I can draw a card from the deck. I need to check, but I think her new score puts her ahead of me.

What is her new score? Who has more miles, Ramona or me?

The skull decorations on these cookies are important symbols of the Day of the Dead.

Deon is next. I know instantly that he has a good card.

> It is late in October and you travel 1,128.1 miles to Oaxaca, Mexico, to participate in Día de los Muertos celebrations. What do English speakers call this important holiday?

"Day of the Dead," Deon says confidently. I check the answer card. Deon is correct.

How many miles does Deon have now?

It is my turn again. I rub my hands together in anticipation. This could be the winning card!

> You ride in a charity bike race. You bike 100 miles from Redmond, Washington, to Granite Falls, north of Seattle. The mountain range near Granite Falls is part of the Ring of Fire. What is the name of this range?

I squeeze my eyes together, listing names of mountain ranges in my head. But I can't think of the answer. "I don't know," I say.

The Cascade Mountain Range runs from British Columbia through Washington, Oregon, and northern California.

"It's the Cascades," Mr. Rivera reminds me.

How disappointing. I couldn't answer the bonus question. So, I earned no miles at all in this round.

South Sister is one of the Three Sisters volcanoes. Scientists think there is a very high threat of a volcanic explosion in the area. The explosion may result in a new volcanic mountain.

MATH AT WORK

Earthquakes

Several of the volcanoes in the Cascade Range are high or very high threats to human safety. So, seismologists study earthquakes to help keep people aware of the danger.

An earthquake's strength, or **magnitude**, depends on how much energy it releases. Seismologists use a scale called the Richter magnitude scale to measure the strength of that energy.

The scale begins at 2 and goes to 9. As the numbers go up, they indicate stronger and stronger earthquakes. A 3.0 earthquake, for example, releases about 31 times more energy than a 2.0 earthquake.

Seismologists use mathematical data to determine what number on the Richter scale to give to an earthquake.

TSUNAMI HAZARD ZONE

IN CASE OF EARTHQUAKE GO TO HIGH GROUND OR INLAND

Tsunamis are sea waves triggered by earthquakes, underwater volcanoes, and landslides. When they are in the open ocean, they are hard to see.

Seismologists also use the data they collect to determine when and where an earthquake is happening. Speedy information can help save people's lives.

For example, an earthquake beneath an ocean can move large amounts of water. This water becomes a series of waves called a **tsunami** (tsoo-NAH-me). Seismologists warn people living in the path of a tsunami so that they can get away from the coast immediately.

Some tsunami waves go unnoticed. Others reach tremendous heights. Imagine a wave as tall as two Eiffel Towers stacked on top of each other. Waves this high struck a bay in Alaska in 1958 after an earthquake that measured 8.3 on the Richter scale.

In 2004, an earthquake in the Indian Ocean measuring 9.2 on the scale produced a tsunami with waves about as tall as the Lincoln Memorial.

Looking Back

Surely, the next round will determine the winner. So, it seems like a good time for a progress check.

Mr. Rivera	3,683.9 miles
Ramona	4,758.4 miles
Deon	4,239.1 miles
B.J.	4,451.7 miles

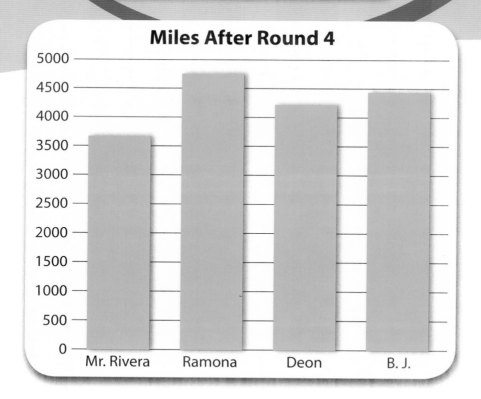

Anyone could win this game.

Mr. Rivera draws a card.

> You travel 332.2 miles from south of Chicago, along Interstate 65. You exit at Mammoth Caves, Kentucky. Inside the caverns, you amble along a trail. These are limestone caves. Needles of rock hang from the ceiling and grow up from the ground. What are these rocky needles called?

Mr. River laughs. "I have a way of remembering this. **Stalactites** are attached to the **c**eiling. **Stalagmites** are attached the **g**round," he says.

I'm going to try to remember that trick myself. How many miles does Mr. Rivera have now?

These stalactites and stalagmites are found in another cave system, Carlsbad Caverns, in New Mexico.

The Rio Grande has carved spectacular canyons through the park.

Next comes Ramona. I squeeze my eyes shut. Is this going to be the winning card?

You travel 473.5 miles from Houston, Texas, to Big Bend National Park. What river forms a 118-mile border between the park and Mexico?

Ramona grins. "It's the Rio Grande," she declares. "My family is planning a camping trip there next spring."

How many miles does Ramona have now?

This turn puts Ramona over the top. The game is over!

But Ramona looks unwilling to end the game. "Why don't we make a new rule? After a player reaches 5,000 miles, the game continues until the round is complete. That way, everyone gets the same number of turns. The player with the most miles wins. What do you think?"

Mr. Rivera says that because it's our game, we should decide. When I see Deon nod his head in agreement, I'm relieved. I could still win this game!

Water erosion creates rock formations like these hoodoos.

On his final turn, Deon chooses this card:

> You travel 720 miles to Bryce Canyon National Park in Utah to see the hoodoos. What are hoodoos?

Deon gets the bonus miles. He knows that **hoodoos** are the towers of rock that stand like totem poles up from the canyon floor.

Deon figures out his score.

How many miles does Deon have in all?

I'm still in the game! I take a card.

> You float down 109 miles of water in a stream that flows from the foothills of the Ozark Mountains. What state are you in?

"Arkansas!" I yell. "Correct," says Mr. Rivera. Then, I total my score.

How many miles do I have in all? Now that the round is over, who has the most miles and wins the game?

This stream flows in the Ozark Mountains in Arkansas.

Mr. Rivera congratulates Ramona on her win. He also congratulates each of us for creating a terrific geography project. Then, he laughs. "I got the lowest score, you know."

"That doesn't mean anything," I tell him. "It's all in the cards. Let me show you what I mean."

I take a card from the deck. "Let's say this had been your card in the last round," I say.

> You're going surfing. Your plane departs Los Angeles, California, and flies 2,563.1 miles to Honolulu, Hawaii's capital. On which of the state's large islands does your plane land?

"Oahu," Mr. Rivera says instantly.

"Do you see what I mean?" I ask him. "At the beginning of the last round, you had 3,683.9 miles. If you had pulled this card, you would have added 2,563.1 miles, plus 100 bonus miles. Let me find the total."

I think about which way I'll find the sum.

Idea 1: I can make a **tally chart**. I can draw 3,683.9 tally marks to show Mr. Rivera's score. Then, I can draw 2,563.1 more tally marks. Next, I can draw an extra 100 tally marks to find the sum.

But tallies work better with small amounts. Drawing so many tally marks will take too long.

Idea 2: I can use base-ten **blocks** and decimal blocks. I enjoy making math models, so this seems like a good choice. But building models of numbers this large will take some time, and I want to find the answer fast.

Idea 3: Writing numbers in **expanded notation** is like untying a knot. It's fun, and I like doing it. I can use this method to solve the problem, but I'm in a hurry. I don't want to make a mistake lining up the place values.

Idea 4: I can use a **place-value chart** like we used in the game. It's simple. It's fast. And I've had lots of practice. I'm going to use this method to find Mr. Rivera's new score.

I use a place-value chart to solve the problem.

I start with Mr. Rivera's score at the end of Round 4. It is 3,683.9 miles.

Then, I add the miles he earned with the new card. That is 2,563.1 miles plus 100 bonus miles.

Would Mr. Rivera have won the game if he had gotten this card instead?

"I see what you mean," Mr. Rivera says. "The cards you draw make a big difference. But that doesn't change the fact that your team has created one of the most challenging geography games I have ever played."

I think Mr. Rivera is exaggerating. But our game is good, I think. I wonder if I can convince everyone to play again.

WHAT COMES NEXT?

Have you ever made a game to test a player's knowledge? You could, you know.

Start by thinking about your favorite class. What is it?

Then, think about the kinds of things you study in this class. List facts that come to mind. You can use these facts to make knowledge cards. You might also want to do some research to find some new facts you don't already know.

Think about how the game will work. Ask yourself questions, such as:

- Why would someone want to play this game?

- Do you want players to do more than answer questions? For example, do you want them to draw pictures or act something out?

- How many players can play at one time?

- Does the game need a game board?

- How long do you want the game to last?

- What must a player do to win the game?

Make a plan first. Then, make the pieces you need. Test your game with friends. It's sure to be fun!

GLOSSARY

addend: a number that is being added.

blocks: Base ten blocks are blocks used to represent numbers through thousands. There are blocks to show ones, tens, hundreds, and thousands. There are also decimal blocks, which are mini-blocks that allow users to manipulate decimal amounts.

difference: the amount that is left when one number is subtracted from another number.

expanded notation: a way to write a number that shows the place value of each digit in the number.

hoodoos: a column of rock left standing after wind and water have eroded nearby rock and soil.

magnitude: the size or strength of an earthquake, as it is measured on a scale such as the Richter Scale.

minuend: the number you subtract from in a subtraction problem. In the problem 12 − 8, the minuend is 12.

operation: an action such as addition, subtraction, multiplication, and division of numbers.

place-value charts: charts that show the place value of each digit in a number.

regrouping: using place value to think of numbers in different ways, such as thinking of 1 ten as 10 ones.

stalactites: a needle of calcite that hangs from the ceiling of a cave.

stalagmites: a needle of calcite that grows upward from the floor of a cave.

subtrahend: the number subtracted from another number in a subtraction problem. In the problem 12 − 8, the subtrahend is 8.

sum: a total, the result of addition.

tally chart: a chart that uses tally marks to count things or events.

tsunami: a series of high waves created by earthquake activity.

FURTHER READING

FICTION

Brighty of the Grand Canyon, by Marguerite Henry, Aladdin, 1991

The Iditarod: The Greatest Win Ever, by Monica Devine, Perfection Learning, 1997

NONFICTION

National Geographic Kids National Parks Guide U.S.A.: The Most Amazing Sights and Cool Activities from Coast to Coast!, by National Geographic Kids, 2012

National Geographic Kids Ultimate U.S. Road Trip Atlas: Maps, Games, Activities, and More for Hours of Backseat Fun, by Crispin Boyer, 2012

ADDITIONAL NOTES

The page references below provide answers to questions asked throughout the book. Questions whose answers will vary are not addressed.

Page 6: 265.4 miles

Page 7: 3,469.0 miles

Page 8: 1,958 miles

Page 9: yes; 937.3 miles

Page 10: Students may say that they'll start in the thousands place and work to the right to determine which number is larger.

Page 12: 299.8 miles; 288.2 miles

Page 13: 2,650.1 miles; 2,550.1 miles

Page 14: 649.5 miles

Page 15: 749.5 miles

Page 16: 2,449.9 miles

Page 17: 467.0 miles

Page 19: 1,904.9 miles

Page 20: 2,822.0 miles

Page 21: 4,349.5 miles

Page 22: 650.5 miles

Page 23: 2,747.0 miles

Page 24: 3,570.7 miles

Page 25: 3,011.0 miles

Page 26: 4,451.7 miles

Page 30: 3,683.9 miles

Page 31: 4,758.4 miles. Ramona has more miles.

Page 32: 4,239.1 miles

Page 37: 4,116.1 miles

Page 38: 5,331.9 miles

Page 40: 5,059.1 miles

Page 41: 4,660.7 miles. Ramona wins the game.

Page 44: Mr. Rivera would have had 6,347.0 miles, putting him far ahead of the rest of the players. He would have won the game.

INDEX

CONTENT CONSULTANT

David T. Hughes

David is an experienced mathematics teacher, writer, presenter, and adviser. He serves as a consultant for the Partnership for Assessment of Readiness for College and Careers. David has also worked as the Senior Program Coordinator for the Charles A. Dana Center at The University of Texas at Austin and was an editor and contributor for the *Mathematics Standards in the Classroom* series.